Enjoying this Magic Mandala Coloring Book?

We would love to hear your feedback and opinions in order to create superior products for you!
Please leave a review and thank you for your support.
Enjoy!

www.ingramcontent.com/pod-product-compliance
Lightning Source LLC
Chambersburg PA
CBHW081556280526
45788CB00011B/3492